8 FEMALE WRITERS / PERFORMERS
# SLAM SPEECHES

Olcan Print
Part of the Olcan Group
London
**www.olcan.co**

First published by Olcan Press on 3rd June 2019
Olcan Print/Press are a subsidiary of the Olcan Group
6 Park Hill, Ealing
London, W5 2JN, UK
Email: team@olcan.co
www.olcan.co

For permission contact:
team@olcan.co

A CIP record of this publication is available from the British Library.
First printed June 2019

Paperback
ISBN: 978-1-9160006-2-9

## FOREWORD FROM THE AUTHORS

Between us, we wanted to create a book of monologues that were different to the other female monologue books we'd seen or read so far. We wanted to create a collection of speeches that introduced compelling characters and told a story within a very short space of time, which is something that Monologue Slam really highlighted for us. It's tricky to get an audience on your side within just one - three minutes however we genuinely believe these speeches will help you to achieve that.

Good luck!

## Monologue Slam UK Foreword

This book is sorely needed. It offers actors a wide range of original, funny, emotive and thought provoking monologues by eight fantastic writer-performers who know first-hand what a great monologue should be.

The team behind the book all have one thing in common; they have all performed at MonologueSlam UK, and for most of them, that's where they started performing their own material.

If you've not heard of MonologueSlam, it's a nationwide, industry supported, showcase for actors. But that sounds a bit dry... Usually when we think of an acting showcase, it takes us right back to our drama schools days, performing monologues and scenes in front of a frighteningly quiet industry audience. MonologueSlam UK is very different...

Open to all, MonologueSlam takes actors through a process of auditions and actor led masterclasses that culminates in an exciting and engaging show with music, a lively host and a guaranteed industry judging panel at every event. Created by actors, for actors, every event is a riotous display of talent in front of a packed out audience in a supportive environment. We've always believed that's where people can do their best, shine and be seen.

Over the past seven years, we've produced MonologueSlams in Birmingham, Coventry, Luton, Cardiff, Colchester, Manchester, Leicester and Newcastle and since it started over 10,000 performers have auditioned, with 1500 performers taking part in a show. We've hosted over 500 industry judges including casting directors such as Amy Hubbard (Lord of the Rings), Julia Crampsie (Head of BBC In House Casting), Tracey Gilham (Catastrophe/Inside No. 9) and Daniel Edwards (Jekyll & Hyde/Mr Selfridge), as well as agents from Independent, Hamilton Hodell and Curtis Brown.

Putting actors directly in front of people in a position to hire them has led to 100's of success stories, including Holby City's Chizzy Akudolu (who now hosts the London show), Kiran Sonia Sawar who received a BAFTA nomination for her role in Charlie Brooker's Black Mirror, Michael Bunani, who started out in the Youth Round and bagged his first agent through the show, going on to book TV roles in shows like Man Down, as well as Aaron Pierre who has starred in American SyFy series Krypton... And of course the wonderful women who have written this book!

But one thing hasn't changed – it's still open to anyone who wants to apply. You don't have to have been to drama school, have an agent, or even have done any acting before. MonologueSlam is part of the TriForce Creative Network and like their other programmes for writers, directors and crew, it aims to increase inclusion in the entertainment industry, making sure people from all walks of life get their shot.

We know it won't be very long before the monologues from this book begin to be performed at MonologueSlam auditions – and we also hope you're inspired to write your own. You can find all upcoming auditions on monologueslam.com – good luck!

*Minnie Ayres*
*TriForce Creative Network*

# THE WRITER/PERFORMERS BEHIND THIS BOOK

## MADELYN SMEDLEY

Madelyn Smedley is an Actress and Writer from Kent. She was selected as a Top Ten Finalist for 'ABC's UK Digital talent contest' in 2017 and 2018. Her TV work includes 'Generation Sext' (Sky Arts) She plays the Estate Agent in the latest NatWest TV advert and can also be seen in the Reese's Pieces and Paddy Power commercials this year. She performed as Helena in A Midsummer Night's Dream at The Brighton Open Air Theatre in 2018 and fell into the moat on press night. She is currently writing a sitcom with her sister Rosie Smedley.

Maddy also sings and plays the acoustic guitar and recently she sang for 'The Mayor at Home' event.

*Madelyn has performed at the London Monologue Slam twice; once in 2017 and again in 2018 as a masterclass winner. Both of these monologues were ones she'd written; Our Night in Dover received a special mention and 'Two For Tuesday' has been performed by a young male actor who competed in the Midland Slams. Both performances can be seen on her YouTube Channel.*

# JOANNA GAY

Joanna is an Actress and Writer from the Midlands. She has appeared in The Archers (BBC Radio 4) and Doctors (BBC1). She has performed in several projects with the Birmingham Rep theatre working in the local community. She will debut her first full length play later this year at the Old Joint Stock theatre. (2019)

*Joanna has performed at Monologue Slam four times; three times in the Birmingham Slams, winning all three times and once in the London Slams; all of which were with self-written pieces. Since then, she has written several monologues for other actors participating in the Slam. She now works with Triforce as part of the team that produce the Midland Slams, auditioning actors and helping things run smoothly at the showcases.*

# KATIE REDFORD

Katie Redford is an Actress and Writer from Nottingham. She was selected for the BBC Writersroom and has since written for stage and screen. She has various scripts in development for TV and has recently written, produced and performed in her first film, 'Ghosted' starring Alison Steadman, which has received backing from the BFI and the National Lottery.

In 2015, she won the BBC Norman Beaton Fellowship and joined The BBC Radio Drama Rep Company. Since, she's worked extensively in Radio Drama and currently plays regular character Lily Pargetter in BBC Radio 4's The Archers. Her TV and film work includes Urban Hymn, Mount Pleasant (Sky 1) Doctors (BBC1) Young Hyacinth (BBC1) and Still Open All Hours. (BBC1)

*Katie has performed at the London Monologue Slam twice; once in 2014 and then again in 2015 with her own written piece.*

# AMBREEN RAZIA

Ambreen is an Actress and Writer from South London. Her critically acclaimed debut play The Diary of a Hounslow Girl, commissioned by Ovalhouse, toured nationally with Black Theatre Live and House Theatre, featured at Alchemy Festival, Southbank and been adapted as a BBC three Pilot featuring on Iplayer. Her second play POT recently finished it's UK national tour. She's also recently finished filming for Netflix.

Awards include Best Newcomer, Asian Media Awards 2016 and Eastern Eye Emerging artist award, 2017. Ambreen was nominated for the Outstanding Achievement Award at the Women of the World in 2017 and won Debut Writer at the 2019 Edinburgh Television Awards.

Ambreen has performed and worked in women's prisons across the UK with companies such as Clean Break. She continues to facilitate workshops with young women, undertaking and discussing issues such as radicalisation, body image, domestic violence, FGM, Girls in Gangs and consent.

*Ambreen performed at the London Monologue Slam in 2014 and won the 1 minute round.*

# DEBRA BAKER

Debra is an Actress and Writer from East London. She's performed at numerous theatres including Soho Theatre, Bristol Tobacco Factory, 59E59 (New York) and Theatre Royal Stratford East. Her TV & Film credits include London Road, Diana, Night Bus, Call the Midwife (BBC1) Coronation Street (ITV) Phoneshop (Ch4) and The Five. (SKY 1) Debra was part of the BBC Radio Drama Company working on many Radio 4 plays and comedies.

Debra started writing in 2016, creating her own project, The Alphabet Monologues, a series of 52 monologues, one for each week of the year. Her first short play, Isabelle, was produced as part of Little Pieces of Gold at The Southwark Playhouse, and then by Drama Studio London as part of their 2018 Showcase. Debra is currently studying Creative Writing (Playwriting & Screenwriting) at City, University of London and is writing her first feature film, due for completion by 2020.

*Debra has performed at the London Monologue Slam twice; once in 2013 and the other in 2016 with her own written piece. Both of which, she won. She was also one of the '10 actors to champion' to be picked by Channel 4 in the end of year Winners Final in December 2016.*

# LAUREN DOUGLIN

Lauren Douglin is an Actress and Writer from Sussex. She began her acting career in TV shows and commercials for Sky 1, Netflix and ITV amongst others after growing up performing in musicals and stage plays in her hometown. Her first short film "Andy & Lucy" began Lauren's journey into screenwriting. This led to her writing bespoke scenes for showreels and progressed on to create the comedy web series City of Dreams alongside character comedian, Scott Hudson. Her next short comedy Two Tyred is currently in pre-production.

She's written comedy pieces for Siberian Lights, Junkbox Theatre and Standing Ovariation using autobiographical experiences to create pieces for comedians, theatre companies and actors alike.

She also works at Central Film School with their directing students showing them the best ways to interact with and direct actors for authentic and dynamic performances.

*Lauren won the online version of Monologue Slam #MonologueMondays, has had her writing used by auditionees and performed in the first Monologue Slam of 2019.*

# STEPH LACEY

Steph Lacey is an Actress and Writer from Peterborough.
She has written two plays, which have both been staged at
53Two in Manchester; Cinder-Chuffin-Rella and To Sleep.
She's about to tour with Taking Flight Theatre Company with
their production of 'Peeling.' She is currently studying for a
PhD, exploring female homelessness and motherhood.

*Steph has performed at the Monologue Slam three times;*
*twice in Birmingham and once in Manchester in 2018, all*
*with self-written pieces.*

# MEG MORTELL

Meg is an Actress and Writer from Gloucestershire. She trained at the Guildford School of Acting. Her credits include The Play that Goes Wrong (West End and UK Tour), Frankenstein (International Tour), Doctors (BBC) and New Tricks (BBC).

Inspired by writing monologues for her experience with monologue slam, Meg wrote a series of monologues and sketches that soon formed into a one woman show 'Lucky Strike' which showcased at The Canal Cafe, Brighton Fringe and then on to Edinburgh Fringe the following year. She is also the co-founder and member of vintage vocal harmony trio, The Femmes.

*Meg performed at the London Monologue Slam in 2013 with her own monologue, which she went on to win. She also went on to win The Winners round the same year.*

# CONTENTS

*These monologues can be performed under any accent, age and gender unless there is something in the piece that obviously specifies any of the above. The current suggestions are just our recommendations but please feel free to tailor them to suit you.*

**Above and Beyond**

**by Steph Lacey**

**Genre: Comedy**

**Age: Any**

**Accent: Northern**

**Length: 3 minutes**

*Donna's disdain for her call centre job is palpable. She despises every customer she is employed to assist as they interrupt the gossip session she comes to work for.*

Good afternoon, you're through to Donna at the Call Centre, how can I help you? Not my department love. No I haven't got a number, sorry. Ok, ta ra love. *(Call ends)*

Have you heard about Jimmy? Have you not? Oh I can't believe you've not heard, it were the talk of the office! Oh it were a right palaver, this woman were kicking off! Proper narky like, chewing Jimmy's ear saying it was his fault she weren't gonna be able to feed her kids and he were like, "No love, it's you not paying your bill what's done that" and so it went on. And you could tell by his face that Jimmy were getting right ticked off with it – or so I'm told - so he puts her on hold, and he goes to town on her, f'in and blindin', calls her a bint, the lot...weren't on hold though were she...Heard the lot, heard the bloody lot. Chuffin' hell! So he's gone. And th- (A call comes through)

---

1

Hello you're through to Donna at the Call Centre, how can I help you? mmhmm, mmhhmm. No, you need to call before 4 for that love, OK? Yep. Ta ra. *(Call ends)*

Anyway, we've got this new lot in, one week in training think they know it all, come and sit next to me, telling me what to do? I don't think so! I- *(Another call comes in)*

*(Increasingly annoyed)* Hello you're through to Donna at the Call Centre, how can I help you? Yeah what's your account number love...mmhhmm... yeah, two secs! I'll get it sent out in writing for you, OK love? Yep, ta ra. (she hangs up)

Let me just put my phone in offline so I don't get another call. Ohhh, I got a rollicking the other day! Chuffin' hell, I tell you what! So, my break were at half 12 right, but Becky's weren't til 12.45, so I thought...I am gonna stretch this call out. So I were giving it all "oh my system's going right slow, do you mind if I pop you on hold?" 5 minutes she were on hold while I were just chatting to Ben. Oh he is fit though, he is. Everyone fancies him though so I don't stand a chance but, nice bit of eye candy. And it's not like there's owt else to look at is there? No offence, I'm not being funny but the rest are grim. It's a good job we're not Skyping them, we'd have no customers left! Anyway, so I goes back to her and I checked every single detail, just to make sure it were "up to date". Above and beyond, me. So then, I go for my lunch and I come back, having sacked of my rota, which normally I'd get away with, but I were late 'cause Nancy in the café upstairs insisted on showing me 644 photos of her grandchildren at school, I mean, the first 4 were lovely, but? So I come back and Jenny's just there, waiting. And she's a right cow, Sharon'll tell you.

*(To Sharon)* Sharon...Sharon. She can't hear me, must be on a call.

**Attack**

**by Debra Baker**

**Genre: Drama**

**Age: 40's to 60's**

**Accent:  Any (Suggestion: RP)**

**Length:  3 minutes**

*A woman in the supermarket recognises an old school colleague*

I'm in Waitrose doing some last-minute shopping for this evening's dinner party.  Alex is at home creating some culinary masterpiece or other, so I've popped out for some more champagne and decide to treat myself to some of those kalamata olives stuffed with feta that I so love, and I look up and there she is...

Jenny Creed.

And I'm stopped in my tracks.  And I'm not sure it's her, because I haven't seen her for, god, it must be well over twenty five years.  But the minute I spot her something in ME changes. I freeze. My breath becomes shallow, rapid... I can feel my heart racing, beating loudly in my ear. I feel sick, hot, cold, confused.  All in a split second.

And yet it's just a woman, standing there, a shop assistant actually, in front of the deli, with a tray of samples.

I glimpse her badge and it does indeed say 'Jenny', so I look again, and it's her, but older, fatter.

'Jenny?' I say and she replies "Yes madam, can I help you?".

'Jenny Creed?' and she looks a bit puzzled and says "Yes?".

"That went to Ferndown Girls School?"

She's more intrigued now. "Yes! Do I know you?"

"It's me, Loveday"

She's searching, thinking. "I remember your name" she says.

"But you don't remember ME? "

"No, not really. Sorry"! An embarrassed laugh escapes her mouth.

"You don't remember me?" I repeat. "You really don't remember me? Are you joking?" I'm louder, more forceful. The vibe has changed. Something in ME has changed. Snapped. She knows it. The balance has shifted.

"You don't remember all the really spiteful things you used to do and say to me?"

She's looking nervous now, not sure what to do.

"All the names? Spoon Shoes? Oh yes, you and your friends used to find that one SO funny! Remember now?"

She starts to shift uncomfortably looking round for someone to help.

"Well I do." I spit the words at her. "I remember every fucking word you said."

And I smash the tray out of her hands. She lets out a small scream. I grab her by the collar and pull her into me. "YOU RUINED MY LIFE!" I shout into her face. I punch her with the full force of my fist. She stumbles back, loses her footing, the deli counter breaking her fall. I'm on her, punching and hitting. She tries to defend herself, but I'm too strong. Years of frustration, imagining this moment, this confrontation, are released.

"Get off me!" she's screaming.

And I'm screaming back "You ruined my life. I hate you!"

From behind I feel big hands grab me and pull me back.

"Madam, are you ok? Madam?" I come to. I'm breathing fast. Shaking. A security guard is holding me. I look up. It's her. Jenny. Her badge tells me so. She's still standing there with her tray of samples. I look into her face. But it's not Jenny Creed. Just a woman with the same name. The name alone has triggered off my anxiety, my panic attack.

'Madam?'

She's waiting for a response, this Jenny. Looking at me concerned.

'Sorry, no I'm fine, thank you'. I stutter. The guard lets go gently.

She smiles. A warm, kind, smile. Proof this is definitely NOT Jenny Creed. 'Well then can I tempt you with some hot smoked trout?'. She proffers the tray.

I back away dazed, trying to get a grip on reality. The phone vibrating in my pocket makes me jump. I take it out and look at the display. Its Alex. My Alex. I'm safe. I answer.

"Hi darling, you still in Waitrose?" he asks chirpily "Could you pick up some truffle oil please"

'Yes of course I will." I say in a strange voice. He hasn't noticed. He's too focused on the dinner

"Thanks darling. Love you". And he hangs up.

I wonder what ever happened to Jenny Creed.

**Awkward meeting**

**by Joanna Gay**

**Genre: Comedy**

**Age: 20's – 30's**

**Length – 3 minutes**

**Accent –Any (suggestion: West Country)**

*Kirsty 'bumps' into Dave outside his work and is confused why he hasn't got back to her after their date.*

You alright Dave? Fancy seeing you here... So weird. Ohhh yeah forgot you worked here, it must have slipped my mind. How are you anyway? I have called a couple of times, text, emailed, poked you on Facebook.

Right what's going on here then Dave? I mean we went on that one amazing date and then I never heard off you again, what's that's about? *(Pause)* Ohhhhh I get what's going on here. Ye happens all the time. Got intimidated didn't ya? Didn't think you could handle this *(points to boobs)* and this *(points to arse)* That's it isn't it? Isn't it? No...? Right are you gay? You've got to be gay that's the only explanation. (pause) Is it because I farted that one time? Cuz I swear to God that that never usually happens, well it happens sometimes... *(starts to shout)* Alright Dave it happens all the time I can't help it I've been to the doctors and everything!

You're not perfect anyway Dave. Dave? *(Coughs under breathe)* shit name. You're fucking boring, and I know your secret Dave, you're a secret ginger, ye don't think I haven't noticed your roots. You're a ginger, lanky minger!

And it's not like you're even funny. No you tell shit jokes. You told me once about an Irish man I laughed but I didn't even get it, it was shit, and I'm pretty sure it was racist.

*(Calms down)* I'm sorry Dave I didn't mean any of that. I got my period this morning and it's just making me a bit fucking mental but that aint your fault and I shouldn't take that out on you. But I mean if you don't actually say anything right now, I will leave. I will walk away. I will. I will walk away. I mean it, speak now or forever hold your peace. I am walking away.

*She Loiters for ages willing him to stop her. She goes to leave...*

Oh come on Dave don't be a dick. *(Starts to laugh)* Look at us, this is soooo us isn't it. You know what this is? Passion. Ye my friends Vicky and Deano never argue but they say that's worse don't they because there no fire there but me and you it's like sparks flying everywhere!

So come on then Dave. Can we just forget all this and go on another date...? Come Dave what do you say? Hmm? *(long silent pause)* Oh sorry, I just farted again.

**Bad day**

**by Joanna Gay**

**Genre: Comedy**

**Age: 20s – 30s**

**Accent: Any (Just not Welsh)**

**Length – 3 minutes**

*Grace has parked illegally whilst she runs an errand.*

No no no! Please don't give me a ticket, I was only 5 minutes. I really needed to park here. I I I I've pulled my hamstring *(she clutches her thigh then hesitantly moves her hands down to her actual hamstring)* Please I've had such a bad day. Sir sir! Madam? Shit I'm so sorry, the beard kind of through me. But hey I mean facial hair is very in right now especially on women. Have you seen The Greatest Showman? bearded lady? Oh Its fantastic. I mean I haven't shaved my vagina in 3 months, yeah why should I? Why should we conform to social pressures? Stick it to em sister!

Anyway please don't give me a ticket I have had the worst time recently. My Mom and Dad have just told me they are deserting me and moving to Wales. Wales! They are basically making me an orphan. I know that might sound over dramatic, but Wales is so fucking far, sorry for swearing, but what the hell is there is Wales? There is nothing to do. Like nothing. I've been there, its shit. The people are so weird, and I swear they're all related. They'll be back. Yep Mom will hate it after a while. She'll be so bored. And the weather! I swear people must have to take vitamin D deficiency tablets due to only seeing the sun three times a god damn year! PLUS my boyfriend thinks I'm overreacting about it all! What does he know? His parents are both dead, he's so lucky. He doesn't know what I'm going through. He said to me the other day he thinks I've let myself go, he said I don't make an effort for him anymore. Oh god I think he's going to dump me. Come to think of it maybe it's the whole unshaved vagina thing...So anyway Miss you can see I really have had a bad time lately so if you can find it within your heart to just let me off this on this occasion that would be amazing *(closely looking at car park attendants name badge)* Mrrr Aled Jones.

**Charity**

**by Debra Baker**

**Genre: Comedy**

**Age:  30's - 60's**

**Accent: Any (Suggested: Strong regional)**

**Length: 3 minutes**

*Hungover Pauline is talking to her friend, who has come for
her fancy dress costume*

Today's going well.  It's eleven o'clock, I'm still in my
pyjamas and have had a doughnut and four choc chip
cookies.  Still, at least I know what colour my aura is (blue),
who would play me in a Hollywood movie of my life (Charlize
Theron.  OBVIOUSLY!) and what my pole dancer name is
(Fluffy von Petto – so that one's your first pet's name, then
VON, then the surname of your first crush (Glen Petto). And
then I started thinking about Glen Petto 'cause he left
secondary school in year nine and I was wondering what he
looked like now.  So I did a little Facebook stalk, but the only
ones I could find were some Neil Diamond tribute from
Canada and a 14 year old in Dumfries.

But I'm hanging. We all got a bit trollied.  It was such a good day yesterday though.  A right laugh.  And we raised just over £380.  Loads more than last year.  Well, we've got the Stevenage office in with us now haven't we. We couldn't wait to see their fancy dress. I mean they're all a little bit odd. Anyway they all came in in pyjamas. The SAME pyjamas! All of them. Like, its not a fucking sleepover its Charity Fancy Dress Day!  Cos with us lot we know each other really well, so you know what everyone's likely to be.  Like you can guarantee James (my boss) will ALWAYS dress up as some sort of superhero (well, he's still a little boy himself really isn't he) Dirty Carol will always come as someone with big tits – just so she can get hers out.  So last year she came as Dolly Parton, this year it was Kim Kardashian, she had the padded arse and everything.  Although she went a bit OTT with the self tan and Raj and Micky kept singing the Oompa Loompa song to her. So those two always come as some sort of 'double act'. This year it was The Krankies, well Micky's only little, isn't he. So they looked really good. Kevin NEVER dresses up, just comes in his usual suit. Boring fucker. So last year we started calling him David Brent and trying to get him to do the dance.   Adrian always comes as a clown, but it's the *same* clown every year. 'Cause apparently that's what he does in his spare time.  Its like, his hobby.  He *is* a clown. I know, right? Sue always comes in in a saucy uniform; saucy nurse, saucy sailor, saucy police officer. And Dave comes dressed as a woman – standard. And then obviously I borrowed your catwoman outfit, yeah thanks for that.

And then yesterday Amanda, the new big boss from Head Office came down. And she'd dressed up as Dorothy from the Wizard of Oz and bought her little dog in with her, really cute. Although most people thought she should have come as the Wicked Witch of the West. But she bought twelve bottles of prosecco in. Trying to win people over! Well we did those really quickly, but we'd got the taste, so then we had a whip round and sent Kevin out to get some more – well he was the only one that looked normal. So yeah we were in the office till about eleven! I don't really remember much of it.

But it was a right laugh. We had the music on, and we were all dancing and singing. Sue and Dave were photocopying their bits. Micky was throwing up in the toilets! Then I slipped over on the way to the loos on what I thought was a coffee spill. Landed right on my arse! But it turned out Amanda's dog had the shits and had done a proper liquidy one right in the corridor. She was proper embarrassed. So she ordered loads of pizza on the company card to make up for it!

So yeah, thank god that catwoman outfit is PVC. Just wiped it right off! It's over there in that bag. Thanks again. Anyway £380 for Children In Need. Result.

**Chattel**
**by Debra Baker**
**Genre: Comedy**
**Age: 30's-50's**
**Accent: Any**
**Length: 3 minutes**

*Harriet moves to a new neighbourhood and finds a new friend.*

I'm slowly stealing my neighbours' cat!

Now this wasn't my intention, you understand. But in all honesty, the cat was the first one to welcome me when I moved in. Well, the only one, if truth be told.

That very first day when I was taking out the packing boxes. There he was in all his fluffy, ginger finery. Wrapping himself around my legs, enticing me with his purring, pleading to be petted.

I couldn't resist. Just gave him a bit of a stroke. Nothing special. That was it.

Next day he's back again. Meowing in the front garden, trying to get my attention. Which of course, he did. I go out, give him a pet. Thought no more about it. Every day he came by, just dropped round casually, like a new friend. Then a couple of weeks later I was at the supermarket and I just happened to find myself down the pet food aisle, so I picked up some cat food, you know, just in case. And the next time I opened the door to him, he waltzed on in.

But it was quite nice, having someone to chat over dinner with. It can be very lonely moving to a new neighbourhood. He is an excellent listener, very good company. Plus, he'd only stay for a few hours.

And he didn't have a collar so I decided to name him Harry, after my favourite ginger, Prince Harry. And of course, I'm Harry too - Harriet. It just felt fated.

And it was all going well, for both of us. He'd pop by every night. It was all very casual and mutual.

Until SHE came over. SHE lives across the road. Lynsey. That's her name. I imagine she spells it L.I.N.Z.I. She's that type.

One Tuesday. There's a loud knock at the door, which surprised me. Nobody ever knocks, except the pizza delivery guy and two lovely ladies from the church, who do the rounds every Sunday. So I answered it and there she was, all loud leggings, contoured face and big hair, like a cheap version of Rupaul.

She says 'Errr, yeah, have you got my cat in there?' and she's glaring at me, her mouth sneering.

'Oh I'm not sure. There is a cat here but I think he's a stray' I say, a bit flustered.

'Big fat ginger thing?' she asks.

'Er yeah'

'He's MINE' she says aggressively. 'Don't let him in again.' Then she calls out 'KANYE, KANYE!' I mean, really! Kanye? Says everything you need to know about HER!

And Harry shoots out the door past her as quick as he can. And I think 'Yeah I don't blame you Harry, she's a nasty piece of work'. I can tell.

So we're careful from then on. I let him in the back door, away from prying eyes and we carry on our nightly routine.

Then one night I don't let him back out after dinner. He stays over.

The next night Lynsey knocks demanding to know where he is. I feign innocence and tell her I haven't seen him. She stomps off towards her house 'I hope you find him!' I call after her. Oh, I'm good!

That was two weeks ago. He stays over most nights now. In my bedroom. Just in case she knocks.

He obviously prefers it here, right?

So tomorrow I'm taking him to the vets. To get him chipped. Let her prove he's her cat then!

**Creases**

**by Katie Redford**

**Genre: Drama**

**Age: 30's**

**Accent: Any**

**Length: 3 minutes**

*Jen visits her family home for the first time since her younger brother's death.*

The cardboard box that the printer came in is still just sitting on the landing because Mum said she wanted to keep hold of it. You know, "Just incase." We don't even have the printer anymore. The framed picture of Les Dennis is still lodged between books on the shelf, which to be fair, I'm pretty relieved about. Dad got it from Mandy in Secret Santa one year and didn't have the heart to say, "Er, what the fuck is this?' Actually Dad wouldn't say fuck. I don't think I've ever heard him say fuck. He's the type of man that will replace a swear word with shit words like "fiddle" and "sugar." He's so jolly. My mates always said he was like Santa. He's hardly said anything since I've been back. He's just been sitting in the shed. Says he's working on something. He's not.

Every time I come home, nothing's changed. All the clutter is still in the same place. Nothing's quite where it should be. But this time, I want everything in the same place. I sort of need everything in the same place .

I knock on his door. Even though I know he's not in.

I dunno whether to sit down on his bed. I don't wanna make a crease in the quilt. If I sit down, I'll crease the quilt, which wasn't there when he was here. And I want everything to be just as it was. So I just stand there, in the middle of his room.  And I get this whiff...this smell of Lynx Africa aftershave. And I'm conflicted 'cause I usually hate that stuff but now, right now, it's the best smell in the world. You forget how powerful smells are. You forget until moments like this. The places they can take you back to.

I'm sat in his room and it's 1998 and he's got this huge Spice Girl poster on his wall behind his TV. Everyone always had a favourite Spice Girl, didn't they? Yeah, he didn't. I used to get so wound up about that. I'd tell him he had to have a favourite Spice Girl and that he was weird if he didn't.

He's got these weird little footballer models on his window ledge. Those little footballer statues where they all had massive heads and massive lips. I nicked his Gary Lineker one and I hid it in my drawer. He was distraught when he noticed that had gone missing. I never gave it back. I'm not sure if he knew I even had it.

Live and Kicking is on the TV. Zoe Ball and Jamie Theakston are there. Legends. And me and him have this massive row because he wants CD:UK on instead so he pulls my hair and I smack him in the arm. I get my own way, even though it's his room. But I was older, so...and then we just sat and watched Live and Kicking and everything was just...

And I'm standing there, in the middle of this room, this badly decorated, but beautifully familiar bedroom and all I can think is how much I want to say sorry. I don't have anything else.

And just when I think that this can't feel any worse, the cat comes in, brushes herself past my leg and jumps on his bed, making a crease in the quilt that wasn't there before.

**Dead honest**
**by Joanna Gay**
**Genre: Drama**
**Age: 30's – 40's**
**Accent – Any**
**Length – 3 minutes**

*Jane is confiding in someone about how she feels about her
late mother.*

I remember thinking that it must just be my imagination. I
was being silly; it couldn't be true.

I replayed past interactions trying to piece together some
sort of explanation. I tried to think back about the first time
my mother met Andrew. I didn't instantly notice anything
out of the ordinary. I mean she was stand offish but he was
my first boyfriend and she was very prudish, it was to be
expected.

Then when we got married, I remember Dad being so happy,
so proud, but she was always so cold. But with Kerry's
boyfriends she was different. Was it because they had better
jobs, or were from better backgrounds or was it because
they were white?

I haven't always agreed with her views. Christ we've had
lengthy debates about politics, films, people we admired but
thinking back now there was always a common factor.

Then we had Jacob and Kerry had Bella. I was so excited to have children at the same time as my sister. They would be the best of friends, the closest cousins they would be practically siblings, and they were. They loved each other, unconditionally. But the love she had for the both of them was different. And again, that internal argument said it was because Jacob was a boy and she wasn't sure how to look after boys. She'd only had daughters and so it was new to her. But I saw the way she looked at him. It wasn't with love, or admiration it was with resentment. She hated taking him out on her own. She never took him to her clubs with her friends and when his afro started to grow, she could barely look at him.

It's kind of ironic that when she collapsed in the supermarket it was a lovely Nigerian lady that drove her to the hospital, and when she got to the hospital it was a wonderful Indian Doctor that tried to save her. And it's taken her death to make me realise exactly what she was.. I just wish I'd have had the courage to tell her when I had the chance.

**Decisions, decisions**
**by Steph Lacey**
**Genre: Drama**
**Age: 20's +**
**Accent: Any**
**Length: 1 minute**

*Nicole is weighing up her donut options in a supermarket. She can't decide and her attention wanders on to more pressing decisions.*

All I want is a bloody donut. An oozing, messy, sugary donut. A simple request, no? A custard one... I know that can be controversial, but the heart wants what it wants. But what have we here? The Krispy Kreme cart of goodness and the world is my oyster. Gone are the days of a simple splodge of custard. Raspberry glaze, apple pie, peanut butter. No, I haven't got a nut allergy, thanks for asking. Christ, for the life of me, I cannot decide. For the 500th time today, my thoughts gather in my belly.

It feels like a parasite, gnawing at me. On some days. On other days I am besotted, ready to love. My baby and me. But it feels wrong. I can't be someone's mummy. But to *do* it means... And everything you think of as a reason to do it or not, as a pro or a con, seems like a judgemental criticism of someone else who made the opposite decision in the same situation.

Oh Christ, who'd have thought donuts would have sent me into an emotional tailspin. I'll get a bloody flapjack.

**Don't Touch The Art**
**by Lauren Douglin**
**Genre: Drama**
**Age: Any**
**Accent: Any**
**Length: 1 minute**

*Kaley is waiting at the bus stop when a stranger in the
queue touches her curly hair*

Did you just pull my hair? I hope you were getting a leaf out
of there.

Ah no you just wanted to touch. Thing is it's attached to my
head.

I know it's soft. A concoction of almond oil, avocado oil,
argan oil and the god given gift that is coconut oil go into
this barnet to keep it fluffy as a cloud.

That and no heat, sleeping on a satin pillow and stopping
strangers shoving their hands in it keep it looking this good.

Can I ask you a question. If I touched your butt because I
wanted to see how soft it was how violated would you feel?

I know, I know it's 'just hair'. But it's mine.

Let me put it this way, you know when you go to an art
gallery and they tell you not to touch the art well this, this is
a masterpiece.

And well we're all masterpieces in our own way. So how
about from now on you go through life like you'd go through
the Tate and don't touch the art.

**Eulogy**
**by Debra Baker**
**Genre: Drama**
**Age: 40's - 60's**
**Accent: Cockney**
**Length: 3 minutes**

*Ange is recounting the story of her dad's funeral to a friend.*

"Go on then, FUCK OFF!!"
Is probably not the most *appropriate* thing to say.
At a funeral.
Just as they're lowering the coffin into the ground.
And it's your dad.
I mean I realise that *now*, in hindsight.
The priest said something about 'appropriate language' and
so of course, I turned into Micky Flanagan and said "Oh no
Father, we're cockney – we don't consider it swearing, its
more like punctuation."
Mum was mortified. I thought my brother was gonna lamp
me one, especially cos his son Billy, who's autistic, then
started chanting "Fuck off, go on fuck off! Fuck off, go on
fuck off!"

But I can understand them being annoyed, they wanted to show their respects. I mean my brother was always his favourite, they used to go fishing and football together and do the stuff that boys and their dads do. Sadly I was born with the wrong genitals! I didn't get to do any of that. And no matter what I did, he wasn't interested and so eventually I just stopped trying to please him.

I think sometimes you're just too much like someone. You know? You're like a mirror, and they just don't like what they see. My mum used to say that an'all 'Oh you're just like your father' which is weird cos she loved *him,* yet *I* never felt that from her. At least with dad, I KNEW he didn't love me. At least he never pretended.

But then he was brought up during the second World War. There wasn't time for emotions then, they were too busy fighting the enemy (and just surviving). I remember him telling me how when he was drafted into the RAF his dad *shook his hand!* And it was the only time they ever made physical contact. My grandad never knew if he would see his son again, and he SHOOK. HIS. HAND. That was all he could muster. So I used that as an excuse for dad not loving me. I justified it!

Anyway I left as soon as I could. I got married and moved out. Didn't really see much of them after that.

Until dad got ill, and that was when things changed.  My brother has to look after Billy, that takes up a lot of his time.  And me mum, she couldn't cope – she fell to pieces and would just go out.  So it was left to me. I was the one who had to take him to appointments, run his errands, and sometimes we'd go down the pub for a pint – well him, not me.  I always think women who drink pints look like lesbians!

 And we finally talked.  You know *really* talked. I mean I could talk to strangers all day long, on the bus, in a supermarket queue.  I'm always chatting to people.  But when it's your own family its quite hard init? But we did talk.  About him. About me.  About life.  About death.

Then one day as I was leaving he said to me "Oh you fucking off now then?"  And I said 'Yeah dad I am'.  He said "Go on then, fuck off!"  And that was what he used to say to me after that, whenever I left.

So that's why it blurted out. Because sometimes its just so much easier to be sarcastic than to actually say what you really want to say to each other, which was …I love you.

**Flutters**
**by Katie Redford**
**Genre: Drama**
**Age: 40's +**
**Accent: Any**
**Length: 3 minutes**

*Grieving the recent loss of her daughter, Kate becomes desperate for a distraction and accepts the challenge of buying a stranger a coffee.*

Anyone else got a picture of Phillip Schofield above their bath?...

Right, no. Well I like him. His face makes me happy. So I framed it. Stu thinks I'm mad but he hates baths, so what does he know?

I don't do anything...y'know...funny... in the bath over Phillip. It's not like that. It's just a nice distraction. You look up - and oooh - hello Phillip. And then back to your bubbles.

Gavi, one of the boys at the co-op, has started setting me tasks. Tasks that distract myself from killing myself basically. I can feel them all watching me at work. Any time anyone mentions children or a child walks into the shop, they all just tense up and look at one another. It's in the air, you can feel it.

*(She gets a list out of her pocket.)*

When he said 'tasks' I thought he meant crosswords, baking, that sort of thing...no. *(Reading)* 'Get on a bus without knowing where it's going' ...which is a bit hard 'cause I've lived here so long, I know where all of them go. *(Reading)* 'Have a cold shower' which if I *was* thinking of killing myself, would tip me over the edge. *(Reading)* 'Write a poem', which I did try, but all I could manage was "The sky is blue, the grass is green, I don't like lettuce but I like ice cream' so...probably won't do that again. *(Reading)* 'Buy a stranger a coffee' which petrified me.

So I'm standing in Pret A Manger - it really annoys Stu when I call it that. He can't understand why I don't just call it Pret. Anyway, I'm standing in this queue and I don't even really want a coffee but it had been another bad morning. I'd been sorting out all of the stuff in her room out...Stu was struggling and I'd already had two baths that morning, so...

Now, you know how in Pret A Manger, the customers line up next to one another as well as in front of one another? Well I can see that there's a man next to me and we both go up to the till and I am so bloody nervous. I haven't felt this nervous since... I'm not sure I've ever felt this nervous. But it's weird, I'm quite thankful for it. Anything to stop thinking. My heart's thumping, my stomach's all over the shop, I'm sweating, my arm pits are soaked and I can't even hear what the lady behind the till is saying to me but all of a sudden, I just blurt out to the man next to me; "I'll get yours!" I've not even looked at him. Keep your eyes down, don't look up because he'll see that you look absolutely insane. I look up at him. And he looks at me like I'm absolutely insane.

But then he smiles. He has a warm, friendly face that even his eyes smile. And if you squint, he looks a bit like Phillip Schofield. I feel something in my stomach. Fluttery. Nothing's really fluttered in me in about 25 years. And I have this urge to just...hug him. *(Tries not to get upset)* I don't want to go back the house and I want to hug him. Really tightly.

And as he sips from his coffee and thanks me again, I realise how unhappy I am. And how much I would like to see the man from Pret A Manger again. As he's walking out the door, he stops and turns back round and tells me it's his turn next time. I smile and make a a weird noise like, "myeha".

And I pray that the flutters last until I get home.

**Hen do's**
**by Katie Redford**
**Genre: Comedy**
**Age: 20's - 30's**
**Accent: Any (Suggestion: Northern)**
**Length: 3 minutes**

*Amy, an out of work actress, is sick of paying for hen do's.*

Well, I found out my agent wasn't dead 'cause I got an audition for a Tango advert.

I'm always skint, so I hate paying for things. I don't mind forking out for things that are standard like ...printer ink...coffees before auditions...coffees after auditions. But do you know what I can't stand paying for? Hen do's.

I went to six last year. SIX. I'm absolutely broke. When my Mum had her hen do, do you know where she went? Pizza Hut. Do you know where Layla went for hers? New York.

The planning, the money, the commitment to actually going - mate, I don't know what I'm doing next week, let alone the third weekend of May in 2022. And don't get me started on the WhatsApp groups. I dread the moment where the bridesmaid pipes up with the part where she tries to bankrupt us all so we can give the bride 'a weekend to remember.' I was genuinely relieved when Shanea settled for Afternoon Tea.

It was downhill from the minute Layla's hen do began. Her, me, Ella, Marnie, Rhiannon and Shiv all met at the airport ready to give Layla this weekend in New York to remember. It were one of them really posh airports - you know it's posh when they've got a Mango - and Ella suggested we all go for a prosecco to start the weekend off. £10 a glass. You could get a bottle and a bit for that in Aldi. But, I didn't want to be that one that couldn't afford it. Plus, they're all dead skinny so they would have been pissed off one glass and the last thing I wanted was to be the only sober one, so I caved. So, we're all sitting in this swanky airport bar and everyone starts chatting about how glad they are to be away from work and they say words like "spreadsheets" and "targets" so by that point, I've switched off. Right, imagine *three* days of that. Three days of listening to them all talk about salaries and promotions and holiday allowances. Talk about the odd one out. Plus, to top it off, Ella were doing Veganuary so every time I had a burger, she'd look at me like I'd shit all over shoe.

When we arrived back at the airport, I was done. Financially and mentally *done.* Within one minute of leaving one another, my phone starts going. It's the pissing WhatsApp group. We've only just left one another and Layla's giving it the whole "You girls are the best - red heart-purple heart-yellow heart" followed by a series of emotional memes from the others and that's it. I've had it. I storm into Sainsburys, look for something that will try and help me calm down and I spend £6 on a Colin the Caterpillar cake. The cashier asks me if I want candles, which is nearly enough to tip me over the edge.

I go and sit on this bench outside the airport where I tuck in to Colin. And it is honestly the happiest I've felt all weekend. Apart from the fact the WhatsApp group is still going off every 5 seconds, which is enough to make me want to hurl my phone at Arrivals. But when I look at my phone, it's not the WhatsApp group. Its's my agent. I got the Tango advert. Fucking buzzing! I look at the dates. They clash. It's Laurie's hen do in Prague.

**Iceland**
**by Meg Mortell**
**Genre: Comedy**
**Age: 20's - 30's**
**Accent: RP**
**Length: 3 minutes**

*Camilla is on the phone to her friend Flick for moral support as she ventures into Iceland.*

Hi Poppet ... I'm in Iceland. Don't ask. Mum fucked the feta dish I was meant to be taking to Penelope's tonight. She was too busy chatting about her new obsession with Paleo that she pored the pissing Prosecco in the pan. Oh I know, I'm literally like how can you be Paleo when you're clearly an alcoholic. So she's having to remake it, whilst I go get my Vajacial, but now she doesn't have time to make the profiteroles so I'm going to just buy some and pretend I made them. I *have* to, I told Patrick they were my signature dish and I'm literally not having him fingering Poppy again. Oh it's got everything to do with fingering darling …
Not being funny but what aisle would profiteroles even be in? Are they frozen? Oh sorry poppet carry on about Freddie, I am listening. Yah, yah ..

Oh my fucking god! *(She has spotted faeces in the middle of the aisle)* No not you sweetie, you're not going to believe this. I can't physically get to my profiter roles because there is a genuine human turd in aisle 3. No I'm not joking, some insane woman is now cordoning off the freezer with her anorak. Does no one work in this piss hole? One sec ... *(She approaches an unenthusiastic member of staff.)*

Excuse me ... You might need to call for a cleaner... like now... I'm not sure if you've noticed but someone has shit on the floor. An actual shit, actually on the floor. Umm I don't really think that sorting the frozen Greggs delivery is a massive ISH right now is it? Mainly because there is an actual Greggs adjacent to this store so why the fuck would someone pop in here to buy a frozen sausage roll? *(To her friend)* Hold on darling.

I don't think you're following me *(looks at her name badge)* Kerry. Oh fucking brilliant. What is this? Does Kerry Katona employ little clones or something? Look, Kerry, this isn't a case of slight soiling or a cheeky guff...Someone has genuinely laid a chocolate log down in front of the dessert freezer. All I need is one box of profiteroles so if you could call for some assistance pronto that'd be super! You can't? Did you hear that Flick, she can't? No Kerry I completely understand that you can't leave your "area" which is...two freezers down from shitgate but do you not have like a walkie talkie or something? ... No. Nope. Of course you don't. Unbelievable. I need one thing...One specific frozen desert. And now thanks to you...Kerry Shitknicks Katona, I certainly won't be getting my profiterole filled with an ounce of Patrick's cream tonight. *(She chucks down her basket)* That's why PRICKS shop at Iceland.

**Inappropriate Boss**

**by Joanna Gay**

**Genre: Comedy**

**Age: 20's – 40's**

**Accent – Any**

**Length – 3 minutes**

*Charlotte has plucked up the courage to confront her boss*

I know you have called this meeting today Martin but before you begin, there is something I need to discuss. This is a little awkward for me actually, I know you are the boss but here goes..

Martin, your behavior around the office at times can be a little inappropriate.

What do I mean? Oh I don't know Martin, how about the email I get every single morning titled 'to do list' and just a picture of your face...No I don't think you send that to everyone in the office as a 'friendly boss banter' Martin. I don't think you send it to Margaret from accounts for example...you know Margaret from accounting. Stinky breathe Margaret? Saggy tits mags. No, didn't think so!
*(She calms back down)*

I mean come on Martin did you really think this was going to happen? I mean I'm... you know *(gestures to her face that she is attractive)* and your, well y-y-you know *(awkwardly gestures he is fat, bold and ugly.)*

I have tried everything to put you off. Last week I even wore men's trousers and a turtleneck. It's June Martin and thirty degrees outside, I nearly fucking died.

I have worked for this company for five years and I will not let you come along and try to belittle everything I have worked for. So enough is enough. No more inappropriate emails, no more offers of shoulder rubs and no more telling me it's tank top Tuesday.... that was very embarrassing for me Martin.

So it stops. Today. Right now. Or I swear to god Martin I will march myself to HR so fast that you will get whiplash.

Are we clear?

*(Shouting)* Martin I said, are we clear?!

Sorry what's that now? R-R-Regional manager....

Oh, oh right...

*(She shamelessly leans forward and pushes her boobs together)*

Well I do hope I am still a consideration.

*(She goes to leave and see's that Margaret from accounting has been sat in the corner of the office. She is mortified.)*

Margaret. Didn't see you there.

**Moles Are A Sign Of Beauty**

**Written by Madelyn Smedley**

**Genre: Comedy**

**Age: Any**

**Accent: Any (Suggestion: Kent/Essex/London)**

**Length: 1 minute**

*Maggie has two hench Moles on her forearm.*

What? Oh... (*Pause*)

...this big thing? Oh.. erm ...It's a mole.

"Oh". He went red. "It's nice"

Thanks

"Sign of beauty, moles"

Made me think it does stick out like a sore thumb... well a sore mole.

What if it is cancerous? You know you hear about skin cancer, it's better to find it early. So, I booked an appointment immediately with Dr Gregson for next Wednesday.

Hi.

"Hi"

I've got some moles that I wanna check.

"Of course, ... Oh yeah, there it is. (Prods and strokes) Let me just measure them too (Gets out his ruler and measures) Yep, they all seem fine. It's the size, if they're more than 7mm and a dodgy shape then we worry"

And I've got two more on my back, I can't see them, obviously, so while I'm here can you check them too please?

"You are really Moley aren't you?"

(I went red)

Yeah. (*Pause*)


I think they're nice.

**Never**
**by Lauren Douglin**
**Genre: Comedy**
**Age: 20's**
**Accent: Any**
**Length: 3 minutes**

*Grace gets caught up in a revealing game of Never Have I Ever.*

My go again? Oh this is hard. Gimme a sec. OK.

Never have I ever been to Zimbabwe.

No one? That's a shame, I hear it's beautiful.

Go on, your go.

*(beat)*

Never have I ever never ever never had sex?

Not gonna lie, I'm a bit confused. Was that a double or a triple negative because if it's a triple then the question doesn't really make sense. Why aren't you looking at everyone else?

Come on shuffle along, we all know we're hoe bags here. Why are you still staring?

Yes wonderful we all now know I'm a virgin - quick, sacrifice me to the mayan gods for summer of healthy crops.

What do you mean why? Honestly it's none of your business what I do with my who who.

Yes I call it a who-who! It's a whole lot nicer than minge caroline.

It's not because I'm a Bible basher, thank you Dom. Well it kind of started that way but some boys make a promise to Jesus then end up in the confessional making out with Joseph. Jesus always forgives. Me on the other hand.

Yeah I wanted to wait until I was married, nothing wrong with that, people marry their Sunday School first love all the time. But alas there is no ring on this finger.

No! This finger has not been anywhere else James you cretin! Because well it's delicate down there isn't it and you never know what you're gonna get. He could have a huge package and well, this sorting station is currently closed.

And what's the deal with bl....you know. Only tasty things should go in your mouth like cake and Nandos, not one of those. Caroline said you just have to treat it like a Mr Whippy on a hot day but if you sneeze you could swallow it whole and there is no way I am going out like that!

And I have not waited 21 years for a let down. Oh Lord, yes Lucy I am 21. I know you had sex with Luke Russell under the climbing frame when you were 13 but I'm not after a gravelly butt. I'm after a loving connection with another human being.

I'm not judging what you do behind closed doors or on your dad's car bonnet, Rich, is your own business.

But to be naked, to be exposed, to be vulnerable,

To literally have another person inside of you... that is not a decision I am willing to make after three tequila shots and a strawpedo too many. So I'll wait. Maybe I'll until I'm 27 or 36 or 49... wait 49 is quite old, my mum's 49, well whenever then, I'll wait.

Yeah maybe I'm scared. What am I saying, I'm terrified but I know I'm gonna be with someone who takes the fear away.

Right if no one's gonna have a go then I will.

Never have I ever been taken up The Shard.

**Never Been Twixxed**

**by Meg Mortell**

**Genre: Comedy**

**Age: 20's**

**Accent: Any (Suggestion: Strong regional)**

**Length: 1 minute**


*Tamla is going on a date and she never goes on dates, so is feeling a little nervous and has come prepared.*
*(She starts by frantically searching her pockets for the list she'd written of conversation starters.)* One sec. It's here somewhere. Tits! Sorry... I'd written a list of conversation starters so I wouldn't make a twat out myself and go off chatting random bollocks on our first date. But turns out all I've managed to bring with me is a... Twix! Well you never know, if you play your cards right, I might let you have a cheeky finger at the end of the night. *(Slowly realises what she's just implied.)* Not like that. Not like that at all. I'm not a slut. I'm not! I was just trying to be nice by letting you have a bit of my Twix and trust me that is a big deal because I don't share with anyone. My problem is...I just love shoving it all it at once. Nothing beats the sensation of having your mouth filled by a big chunk of chocolate.I didn't mean that to sound like ... Because I mean, I don't actually have a preference in colour. Using that train of thought...I'd just as happily have a Milky Bar as I would a Bournville or even better...Caramac. *(Deep breath, followed by an awkward pause. She holds out the Twix)* Twix?

**Oh Knickers!**

**by Steph Lacey**

**Genre: Comedy/Drama**

**Age: 18 +**

**Accent: Any**

**Length: 3 minutes**

*Jennifer, an electric wheelchair user, is enjoying a cuppa and a gossip with her best friend when an unexpected knock at the door throws her off track.*

Who's that knocking on my door? I'm not expecting anyone? I've got my knickers drying on the door handles! They're not even me good knickers, I don't know if I'd mind if I had my lacy ones scattered around, I mean, I wouldn't invite anyone round to look or anything but I'd be more relaxed than the thought of someone walking in to these monstrosities, these parachutes adorning my doors like some perverted kind of swingers Christmas decorations.

Knickers are weird, aren't they? Have you ever given that much thought, how the knickers you wear can change your whole demeanour? So, I've got these ones that are hanging on my handles now that I don't want anyone to see but they are the comfiest things in the world. The energy I get from these pants is unreal. I can pull them over my rolls, tuck it all in, they keep me snug, they don't wiggle down when I move...

Then I've got those ones I wouldn't mind getting down to, the ones that make me feel like I've got a little secret, a bit cheeky, but they cut me in half like one of those wire cheese cutters. As soon as I move an inch, up they go and I've gotta sit there with a smile painted on my face, pretending that I'm not being hung, drawn and quartered by my own undies.

Who'd have thought I'd be sat here, on a Tuesday morning, contemplating the politics of knickers. But it's something that needs thinking about... Yes they keep your toots warm, provide some basic hygiene, prevent some significant chaffage; but they're so much more than what they actually are.

People assume I'm the Virgin bloody Mary cause I'm in a chair, but let me tell you, I am down to...Well, sometimes, depending on the person and my mood and the general ambience really. But sometimes. Not always. Not even every time I've got a matching set on which, I'll admit isn't all that often. *(Beat. Then the thoughts come pouring out.)* But sometimes there's that time when you meet this fella and you go for a drink and you get on and you think 'he's alright' and then suddenly he's all over you and he won't stop. Nature's fucking weapon, hard and unrelenting. You can feel it pressing on you and you can sense the moment is coming and there is nothing you can do. You claw at his face to try and get him to get off. Go away. Fuck off. But because he's mauled at your clothes and seen the lace he assumes he's in. He's turned your power off to your chair and holds your arms behind your back. It's not for you. It's not fucking for you!

*(Beat. Back to light-hearted)* Ooh sorry I've gone a bit deep there. Has your tea gone cold? I'll fetch another. Ooh, at least the knocking's stopped, I wonder who it was. Oh, you don't mind the knickers, do you? I didn't even think to worry about you, sorry. Wanna biscuit?

**Our Night In Dover**

**by Madelyn Smedley**

**Genre: Comedy/Drama**

**Age: Any**

**Accent: Any (Suggestion: Kent/London/Essex)**

**Length: 1/3 minutes**


*Maddy recounts her love for Terry to her best friend Jackie. (Hums the line: "There'll be blue birds over the white cliffs of Dover tomorrow, just you wait and see" from the song White Cliffs of Dover by Vera Lynn)*

...I felt like Vera Lynn but with a little bit of dementia cos I could only remember the first line.

We went for a romantic getaway. Terry had a voucher. I called him Terry because basically he looked like John Terry and I remember showing my brother a picture and I was like "This is me and John Terry" and he was like "He looks nothing like John Terry!" So from then on I just called him Terry.

Anyway. 3 course Meal. Avant Gardè menu.

I even bought sexy underwear for the evening bit. So, I run to the bathroom and slip it on. I was so embarrassed.

"You alright in there?"

"Yeah!... Yeah, I'll be right with you Terry. Don't you go doing a runner Terry!" *(laughs)* Thought I'd lighten the mood.

Then I come out.

"Surprise!"

HE GOT A BONER STRAIGHT AWAY.

Since our night in Dover he kept buying me matching pairs!

*(Pause)*

Terry's not with us anymore.

But when I go to Dover I stare at the sea an it's like a million floating diamonds and I feel like... like a millionaire.

And Terry's there with me. *(Pause)*

And guess what?

I'm wearing my nice pants

and I know he's pleased to see me.

**Pharell**

**by Katie Redford**

**Genre: Comedy**

**Age: Any**

**Accent: Northern**

**Length: 1 minute**

*Janie's obsession with Pharell Williams gets slightly out of hand when she finally gets to meet him.*

Clap your hands if you feel like a room without a roof...Yeah, I don't get it either. How can you feel like a room without a roof? I don't even feel like a room with a roof. Plus, rooms can't clap. I just don't think he's thought it through...

That were one of the things I'd planned to ask Pharell. He were doing some massive charity appearance for Help the Heroes at t'big ASDA in town, which I thought were dead good of him.

I couldn't decide what to wear but I went for yellow cos yellow's a happy colour and he's always banging on about being happy, int he? I'd also put together a little dance routine for him too. Nothing special, y'know, just a few moves to brighten up his day. (I would show you but I've hurt me back.) I'd also made him a little chocolate cake and I were planning on icing it with "I have a spaceship you want to ride" but I ran out of room so it just said, "I have a spaceship." Which were odd 'cause I've never had a spaceship.

Anyway, there I am outside ASDA in this massive queue and this car pulls up and it's him! It's actually HIM! So I just start charging towards him. Now, I'm not a violent person me but I were elbowing and shoving people left, right and centre just to get to t'front. And then I see him clock me! He clocks me running towards him! I think, deep down, he were flattered but he covered it up by looking absolutely fucking petrified. I'm getting closer and closer and closer to him, and before I know it, I'm touching him! Me! Touching Pharell of t' tele! And then I don't really know what happened, it's all a bit of a blur, but... I bit him. I bit his whole hand and I know I shouldn't have done... but its Pharell of the tele.

And as the security guards are dragging me away, I look at Pharell off the tele and I know deep down, he's happy...again. And that he feels like a room without a roof. Whatever that actually even means.

**POT**

**by Ambreen Razia**

**Genre: Drama**

**Age: Teens / Early 20's**

**Accent: London**

**Length: 1 minute**

*Louisa tells Miles how she and Josh tortured young Shanice.*

You wanna know what happened?

We talked.

We talked about the first time we met, when Josh saw me smokin' outside my hostel, the first time he blessed my feet with new kicks and told me that he was gonna look after me, that no one would ever touch me.

We spoke about our plans, what trips what we were gonna take, baby names. We did it together, we mapped out everythin' and nothin' else mattered, not Mark not payback, just gettin' out.

When I went back to her it was easy, just a job. I think she could see that too, I looked at her and she had accepted it...

She looked like a proper soldier and I had more respect for her then.

And I just got on with it.

I didn't hear anything except my own breath. I didn't feel a push or a tug or feel any kind of need to stop. Her crimped black hair stickin' to the side of her face all matted up, held up by the around her mouth, the dirt underneath her fingernails, her white trainers covered in mud.

And me,

me standin' over her like a fuckin' hunter!

I was God.

**Roam**

**by Debra Baker**

**Genre: Drama**

**Age: 50's +**

**Accent: Any**

**Length:  3 minutes**


*Babs is on a park bench, recounting her travels to a stranger.*

I should have thrown a coin in the fountain.  That's what they say; throw a coin in the Trevi Fountain and you'll return to Rome.  But I never did.  Have you been?  Oh the fountain is wonderful.  Majestic statues with the rush of the water filling your ears, making it feel as though the carved horses will stampede off at any moment.

But my favourite site was the Pantheon.  I was just nineteen when I set out on my first trip abroad.  I was studying at the University of Liverpool and was going on a student exchange to Italy.  It was all very exciting.  The family I was staying with suggested the Pantheon.  I remember battling my way through the traffic and noise to get there and as soon I entered through the huge oak door, everything just disappeared; the noise, the bustle, the stress of the world. It's such a calm and beautiful place and the domed ceiling is so incredible in scale that your eyes naturally drift up to the centrepiece; the oculus, the opening, the gateway to God. And you really do feel, almost SEE his presence there.  It is a very special place.  I felt at home, I felt love.

And that is how it all started – my travels. Well I sent a letter back to my mother all about Rome, who showed it to a friend, whose uncle was a newspaper editor and on my return I was invited to his office. So after a lengthy conversation, (I didn't realise it was an interview) I was asked to work on the travel section. Well of course I was flattered. What an honour, especially for a *woman* and so I immediately accepted. But they just loved my writing. And that's how my pieces were published – as letters home to my mother. 'Dear Mother' was the name of the article. Did you ever read them?

Oh, what a wonderful career I had. I visited all the continents and 92 countries. I've stayed with a Bedouin tribe in the Yemen, calved lambs in Wales, wrote poetry at the Taj Mahal, was proposed to at the Empire State Building, swam with turtles in Hawaii, made love to a Berber goat herder in the Atlas Mountains, ate snake in the Australian outback and hot air ballooned over the Gobi Desert.

And people often ask me where my favourite place is. And I always tell them 'Right here. In this park, on this bench'.

For this is where I met my husband, Tom,. And even after we were married, I would still go off on my travels but when I came back, we would always come here. I would tell him all about my adventures. And when I was finished, he would look at me with those soft blue eyes of his and say 'I'm glad you're home Babs'.

And he was home. To me. With him I found that same feeling that I felt at The Pantheon that time.

That feeling of peace.

Of love.

But sadly he's been gone for several years now.

Maybe its about time I started to organise another trip to Rome.

**RTA**

**by Lauren Douglin**

**Genre: Comedy**

**Age: Any**

**Accent: Any (Suggested: Strong regional)**

**Length: 3 minutes**

*Alice nabs herself a seat on a busy train. After a few moments of silence, her phone buzzes.*

Hi babe, how did it go?

What do you mean you never made it?

Slow down, slow down, are you ok?

Michelle. I can't understand you when you're crying. Babe, take a breath. Remember what Guru Maguthta says - channel the energy through your air flow. Breathe in peace, let the darkness go. Michelle. You're not channelling your flow. Will you just take a breath!

What do you mean you've had an accident?!

Is it serious? Are you hurt?

Michelle, babe. What do you mean you hit him?

You hit him with your car? I told you not to take those country lanes.

Ah shit Meesh what have you done?!

Oh God! No I didn't mean it like that. Of course he came out of nowhere. You Lewis Hamilton driving was never setting you up for an accident.

Sorry, sorry. I know. I'm not helping. Ok well where is he now?

In the middle of the road?! Is he breathing?

Well you need to go and check.

Well you go up to him and listen for breath. See if his chest is going up and down... Well is he?

For Christ's sake! Bloody tunnels!

Michelle!

Oh my God Michelle. Are you telling me...

Oh Jesus he's dead! You've gotta call for help.

You won't go to prison, it was an accident.

OK. Ok. Well then you'll have to get rid of the body,  you can't leave it in the middle of the road. There must be a ditch you could kick it into. Well if you're wearing you Loubs just take them off. Kickboxercise finally comes in handy.

Sorry, sorry, I know it's no laughing matter.

What do you mean someone's coming?

What is it with these bloody tunnels!?

Michelle! Did they see you?

So you just laid over the body. Good move. They'll just think you're having a moment- no witnesses.

You've got him in the ditch. Well done babe I am so proud of you. I can't imagine what you're going through. Just throw some twigs and Moss over him. Give him a decent burial.

You want to say a prayer. I don't know any bloody prayers. I learnt this one at school:

"For the food we are about to receive, may the Lord make us truly grateful."

No I'm not telling you to eat him but it was short notice!
Right babe my stop's next so I can meet you at yours in 15
mins - I'll bring a bottle of Rioja to calm your nerves and
toast his spirit.
I hope he didn't have a family. Sorry! Me and my big mouth.
Of course he didn't. He wouldn't have been so reckless in the
road if he did.
Right love. I'm getting off get back in the car and I'll see you
in a mo. Love you babe.
(Exits train)
Poor bloody squirrel.

**Saggy Maggy**

**by Meg Mortell**

**Genre: Comedy**

**Age: 20's**

**Accent: Any (Suggestion: West Country)**

**Length: 1 minute**

*Phoebe is a cleaner at her local rec centre. She's had enough and bursts into her manager's office to explain how she's feeling.*

Look. I'm not being funny but a bit too much malting has been going on in the changing room recently. And I don't just mean head hair. It is pubes galore in them showers. And as for the modesty! Why do women of a certain age feel it's ok to parade around baring all? Cos' I don't know about you but I feel that once (gestures to her boobs) gravity has taken its toll and you have let nature (gestures down below) run its course... Then you should also learn the real use for a fuckin' towel! And that is not cocking your leg up on the side and using it to floss your flaps. This morning, when I was getting on with my chores in ladies changing room. Old Maggy struts in and she just drops her towel. BOOSH! (Mimes throwing her towel down) Then she goes "Scuse the Foof". Scuse it? SCUSE IT? I am on the floor scrubbing so it's in my bloody face. Eleven o'clock on a Monday morning and I am on all fours with a face full of...droopy ... Biff! (Gathers herself for her big finish) So excuse my language and my explicit story but I've basically come to tell you that I'm leaving. I'm throwing my towel in. Just like Saggy Maggy!

**Set Free**
**by Joanna Gay**
**Genre: Drama**
**Age: 40's - 60's**
**Accent:  Any**
**Length: 1 minute**

My son will die in one weeks' time. I know it and he knows it. He is so precious and so complex that he has found this world too hard. And so I have done the hardest thing any mother will ever do. I have accepted that he doesn't want to be here anymore.

David first tried to end his life 3 years ago. He had taken an overdose and needed his stomach pumped. Then a year later, he tried to hang himself. I wake up every morning, terrified that I will go into his bedroom and he will have done it again. So six months ago I sat him down and asked him the question "Do you want to live?" And although the answer was heart breaking, I said "OK, well then, I have a proposal. Can you please give me six months to accept it, six months to plan it and six months where I can go to sleep every night and know my beautiful baby boy will still be there in the morning. He accepted my request and strangely the last few months I have seen him the happiest I've ever seen him, it's like he knew there was light at the end of the tunnel. We've laughed, we've talked, and he's explained things to me that I admit I don't understand but I do have to accept.

So we are one week away. That date on my calendar has been silently creeping closer and closer like a storm you can see in the distance and soon that storm will be in my past rather than in my future. Arrangements have been made and this time David won't fail. I will kiss him on his head the night before, tell him I love him and that will be that.

In one weeks' time, my son will kill himself but he will be set free.

**Sex Education**

**by Meg Mortell**

**Genre: Comedy**

**Age: 20's**

**Accent:  Any (Suggestion: West Country)**

**Length: 3 minutes**

*Shaz is a cleaner at a secondary school. She's been asked to supervise a year 7 class as the teacher is running late.*

Alright year 7...Mrs Robbins is running late so I'm supervising 'till she gets here. But might as well help her out and get you started. And today's topic is *(Looks behind her the board)* Sex Education. Well, fuck me! Well don't, don't actually 'cause...that would be illegal. Anyway...my name's Miss Parge *(Awkwardly straddles a chair but swiftly changes her mind)* so any questions don't hesitate to...say my name *(Gestures riding a horse)* What's my name bitch! *(Starts to panic.)*

Sorry. I'm just really nervous. 'Cause, to be fair, you lot probably know more about sex than I do by looking at you. I mean I can't remember the last time I had sex. *(Cocks up a leg on the chair)* Dry as Ghandi's flip flop down there. *(Awkwardly removes leg from chair.)*

Anyone preggers? You sure? You look pretty... *(Gestures pregnant belly.)*

No? Good. Umm...I know! Let's have a little quiz. Right, ok...one for the girls first. If you share bath water with someone of the opposite sex...can that make you pregnant? No, correct. You could catch aids though... That was a joke. Right, got it - one for the boys. Hands up if you think you can tell the size of a man's todger by looking at his feet? Wrong. And I will tell you why. This boy Kevin in my year at school, right, had size 14 feet. Huge they were. Everyone wanted a slice. Turned out Kevin...actually had a vagina, so... Ok, last one, last one. Is it ok to be 'spontaneous' sexually without the permission of your partner? Wrong. It is not ok. Because if, for example, they decide to spice things up and I dunno...spray whipped cream, all over you and when turning on the light to work out what the smell is...I find myself covered in gone off cream, I can assure you *(wells up)* it will not be dickhead Dave that gets called 'mouldy tits' for the rest of his life, will it?

*(Looks at the class trying to read their faces. Suddenly realising...)*

Oh hello Miss Robbins...I was just telling them about

*(gestures to the board / sexual gesture)*

'Cause it's sex education.

(She swiftly exits.)

**The Diary of a Hounslow Girl**

**by Ambreen Razia**

**Genre: Drama**

**Age: Late teens - 20's**

**Accent: London**

**Length: 3 minutes**


*Shaheeda grips her suitcase and stands by her bedroom door. Before leaving she turns back and addresses the audience.*

I know what you're thinking; I know what you're thinking! 'Hounslow Girl'... A lost little Hounslow Girl with no real prospects or grip on reality and I can see it written all over your faces! I might have known what I was gonna do all along but I ain't lied about anything, maybe I told you too much but I couldn't just tell you the basics or you'll just chalk me up as another Tracey Brooker which I know you wanna do, coz it will be easier and we all know that there's a better chance that I'm guaranteed happiness out there! I'm guaranteed first-hand wisdom and I can actually be taught something without someone having to teach me, coz I've come to realise that you don't really learn anything real from people, and I still have all these questions that no one here has the answer to! And I ain't got time to answer them myself because that's what I've been doing here this whole time, answering my own questions! And that's all I've got coming my way. Questions about this year, about the future about life! And I ain't lived mine so don't ask me.

I don't care if Allah ever forgives me for this, coz I can feel you breathing down my neck right about now. I don't care if you ever forgive me! Because you're the one who put me in this mess! It's your entire fault. I mean what is this obsession you have with giving people happiness and then snatching it away? I don't need someone else to tell me about the Seven Wonders of the World and how I'm gonna feel when I'm stood in front of them. I mean who actually decided on the Seven Wonders of the World in the first place? Some philosopher of some kind decided that Niagara Falls is more beautiful than the marble caverns in Chile, or the Great Wall of China is more breath taking than the Shara Bridge in Yemen! From the Great Pyramid of Geeza to the Northern Lights! Whatever! They were built by people! They were built by people, people who can recognise beauty! People who felt like they needed something exquisite so it could distract them from the boring places that you created in the first place! I mean I used to speak to Uncle about the Seven Wonders of the World and he was convinced that Mecca was one of them, innit? I used to have to tell him, 'Bruv', it's really not.

But to him it was.

To See, To Hear, To Touch, To Taste, To Feel, To Love. To live.

Could they be the true Seven Wonders of the World?

*(Beat)*

I'll stay, I'll face her, face this and give it all a go.

*(Beat)*

I know growing up starts with taking some kind of responsibility and seeking forgiveness from those you've hurt. From the people who are here... from her. Her who looked after us and tried her best to protect us, her who carries paradise beneath her feet like Uncle Abdul Azeez says that all mothers do and I don't think I could have ever really seen it through her eyes until now... now I realise that paradise will soon be beneath mine.

*(Shaheeda looks around her room)*

(Beat)

*(she places her suitcase beneath her bed.)*

(Beat)

The feelings I have now won't disappear overnight, but somehow, someway.... everything will be alright.

*(She sits on the bed and faces her bedroom door, preparing herself for what's about to come through it. She catches the audience looking at her and addresses them one last time.)*

I ain't dumb. I'm intelligent enough to know, that I don't know anything.

And do you know what?

I think that might get me through.

**The Canary Wharf**

**by Madelyn Smedley**

**Genre: Comedy/drama**

**Age: 20's**

**Accent: Any (Suggestion: Kent/London/Essex)**

**Length: 1 minute**

*Molly is at the bus stop with her best friend Rose, who suffers from depression.*

You know, if you go up to the top of the hill, by the Chinese, then do a left, then a right, left, then do another left, then do another left than a right then you get to that big hill you know er... near KFC opposite McDonald's, near the chippy. Yeah.  Well on that hill if you look out... you can see that big flashing building in London.

Poppy said I was lying but you can, if you squint really hard, like that, for about 5 minutes. You can see whatever you wanna see. Although I am a bit short sited.

*(Pause)*

But If you really search for something, you'll find it eventually that's what I always say.

I got 24 % in my final dissertation, so I went and stood on that hill. It made me feel better.

A little bit.

The Canary Wharf looks really pretty in the dark like a Christmas light that's been left on all year.

Sorry... I'm tryna think of ways to make you happy again. Do you wanna stand on the hill with me? ...KFC?

(*Pause*)

Cup of tea?...

I'll make you one. You can have 3 digestives; I wouldn't tell. I've got the ones you know the ones with the caramel in the middle. They're really nice.

You know, you give off a good... No not scent (*smiles*) ...a good, vibe.

And, I'm here, If... if you ever wanna chat.

**This Lily**
**by Katie Redford**
**Genre: Comedy/Drama**
**Age: 20's**
**Accent: Northern**
**Length: 3 minutes**

*Maddy's had enough of her nannying shifts and when she's pushed over the edge by 8 year old Lily, she suddenly sees red.*

(SHOUTS) "Mummy! We're out of avo's!"

It's 5pm. 2 more hours to go. There are worse jobs than nannying, I know. But it doesn't half grind you down. Especially when the kids are little shits. At least I'm in a proper lavish pad. And it really is lavish. It's the type of house that has mugs that are all the same style. Not like the ones we have back home. There's always a part of me that dies inside a bit when we have guests round and Mum hands over their brew in a "Fifa 98" mug.

Lily's rooting through the fridge. She huffs a few times and then slams the door shut. I know she wants my attention, but I'm not gonna give it to her. If I've learnt anything from watching Super Nanny, it's that.

She huffs a bit more. I give in. But only because I don't know what else will pass the time.

"What's the matter Lils?"

She narrows her eyes at me.

"It's *Lily*."

I think about putting my foot out so she trips and catches her head slightly on the work top. Nothing serious, like. Just enough to give her a bit of a wake up call.

"I'm starving." she says, throwing her 8 year old head back like she's got all the troubles in the world.

"You know Lily, there are actually people out there who are *dying* from starvation. You my friend, are not one of them."

"Your voice is *so* weird." she says, head now buried in her iPad.

"It's not weird. I'm just from a different place to you, that's all."

She rolls her eyes. Something she's only started doing recently and it's infuriating.

"I'm from the North." I dry some of the unified mugs so I look busy incase her Mum comes home.

She makes this high pitched "hmph" sound, goes to walk out of the room and says:

"That would explain why you have holes in your shoes."

I actually want to punch her. And I've never wanted to punch an 8 year old. Listen, I hold my hands up, I'm not a saint. I've done bad things, y'know, I've shop lifted...not properly, only from like, Superdrug but I'm not an *evil* person. Yet this girl...this Lily. She makes me want to commit a crime. A proper crime.

I look down at my shoes, which I probably shouldn't have on in the house, but...anyway it's not a hole. It's a gap. A gap that Sinead made when we had that night out in Bradford and we got carried away dancing to 90's megamix.

I go to the drawer, take out the sharpest kitchen scissors I can find and I follow Lily out of the room. When I reach the stairs, she's already at the top of them and shuts herself in her room. There, on the floor in front of me, are her neatly placed school shoes. I pick one up and without hesitating, I plunge the scissors into the sole of them. The leathers quite tricky but I give it a good go. I'll show her what a fucking hole looks like.

And then Mum walks through the front door. She's on the phone but cups it then she sees me. God forbid whoever she's on the phone to, hears a voice from the noth.

"What are you doing?"

I freeze. With Lily's shoe in one hand and the scissors in the other.

I literally don't know what to say. I muster up all I can think of. "Art."

What do you mean, "Art"?

"H...Homework. Lily's art homework."

Her mum glares at me and I'm not sure if she's going to call the Police or just fire me there and then. But she doesn't do either. She makes the same "hmph" noise and says summit about, "the fucking curriculum" and goes back to her phone call, walks past me and slams the lounge door shut behind her.

And then I have this thought.  This thought that scares the shit out of me. I stand at the bottom of the stairs, in this house where as far as I'm aware, everyone needs to learn a lesson, and I'm scared because I'm suddenly now very aware of just how oblivious everyone in this house actually is.

And then I climb the stairs.

**Three Tequilas**
**by Lauren Douglin**
**Genre: Drama**
**Age: 20s – 30s**
**Accent: Any**
**Length: 1 minute**

*Vicky is explaining to her Nan why her engagement has ended.*

I just can't take it off yet.

No not because I have chubby fingers Nana. But once it's off, well, it's off. I know I'm 'getting on' but just so you know twenty eight isn't past it. I could still find someone. If someone else wants me.

It wasn't his fault, it was mine. He didn't cheat. I didn't cheat. Just things changed. What we wanted changed. Saving myself for marriage would have not solved the issue Nana. If Jesus was that concerned he would have intervened after the third tequila shot on our fourth date. It just took us three years to realise that our paths would divert.

Losing the venue deposit doesn't really matter. It's just money and if anything we can use it for your eightieth if it bothers you that much.

It's not his fault, sometimes people just want different things. It's just easier to say I didn't want them rather than I can't have them. But now he can. And I know he'll make a great Dad.

**Thumper**

**by Steph Lacey**

**Genre: Drama**

**Age: Late teens - 20's**

**Accent: Any**

**Length: 3 minutes**

*Lauren, a recently disabled woman is coming to terms with her illness, needing carers, and the surprises that it brings.*

The thing is though, there was a dead rabbit. A dead...rabbit. A fucking dead rabbit. On the bedroom floor. Near me. There. I watched it die. Twerking its poor little tail on the way out. Have you ever had to explain that to anyone? A bloody dead rabbit on your floor? I mean, it's not like I killed it or anything, the cat brought it in, but I imagine it's still quite the sight to behold if you're the carer walking into it. She was alright actually, Brenda. Took it all in her stride. She used to wake me up with a "Morning Princess" or a "Rise and shine little light of mine". I liked those days. I was less enamoured by Carol who used to dip her yellow, tobacco stained fingers right into the milk of my Cinnamon Grahams because she'd "never tried them before". Yesterday doesn't count then Carol, no?

It's a weird thing to suddenly need carers. To rely so completely on another human being when you were convinced you'd handle this life thing alone. I mean, I was so fiercely independent that I'd actually confined myself to loneliness a bit, convinced I could take it all in myself. So it was an odd shift to go from that to have to need someone lift up your boobies to have a wash. It comes to something doesn't it, when your ultimate dream is to have a piss without having to announce it to anyone. I was angry about it at first, it felt unfair. Especially when they took my bed away and made me sleep in a hospital bed. That stung most and I still can't work out why. Like I wasn't a person anymore I guess. Just a patient. Just my illness and nothing more.

Why me? I used to think that a lot. Why me? Well why not? What makes me think I'm so special that nothing can touch me? Why should I be impenetrable to shit? Well, I'm not, clearly. You get used to it though, don't you? Whatever happens. I had a new carer the other day, I can't remember her name, I haven't made up my mind about her yet. But she seemed so surprised that I was happy. That I wasn't wallowing in self-pity. She said she'd pray for me, that she hated to see a life so young wasted. But I wanted to shout: it's not wasted. That rabbit, that was a life wasted. But mine is ahead of me, mine is going to be whatever I damn well please, mine is going to be full of joy and laughter and love and sex and whatever else my bloody heart desires. So thank you for your prayers, but...I'm good.

**Two for Tuesday**

**by Madelyn Smedley**

**Genre: Comedy**

**Age: Teens - 20's**

**Accent: Any (Suggestion: Kent/London/Essex)**

**Length: 1 minute**

*Marge confides in her friend Simon, in the lounge on the sofa.*

So, I get to this party and they're making me down this dirty pint and it's making me gag a little bit in my mouth, so I run to the toilets then I'm gagging in the toilets then I'm sick in the toilet, then I come out the toilets and I say to myself just stick to Rosé.

Then I see this guy, big black man, he's gorgeous! and he says, "Can I take you Nandos?" and I was like "Yeah, alright".

I played it so cool.

So, he takes me Nandos and one thing led to another and well...

I didn't tell him I was a virgin.

But I think he could tell.

And this morning I wake up and I'm singing Justin Bieber.

*(Her phone goes off)*

Oo Miss Popular...

*(Pause)*

It's Dominoes.

*(Pause)*

Two for Tuesday.

I don't really fancy a pizza. I didn't even get his name.

**War Wounds**

**by Lauren Douglin**

**Genre: Comedy**

**Age: 20's - 40's**

**Accent: Any**

**Length: 3 minutes**

*Maggie has brought home Jay for a one-night stand but it doesn't go as planned when he body shames her.*

OK, Jay, you might be drunk, I might be drunk...No wait I'm definitely drunk but this, this is gonna be amazing. I haven't been eyeing you up for a month for nothing.

*(Maggie lifts her top)*

What's this?

It's my tummy. You've got one as well. My belly button?

Oh this. Err it's um...Well it's a....a stab wound?

You think this is a stab wound? Why in Gods name do you think this is a stab wound?

Do I look like I've been in some sort of gang warfare? I work in insurance.

It's a stretch mark fool.

NO. I haven't had a baby. You've known me for weeks and I have never once mentioned kids. Let's engage the brain, shall we?

You don't just get stretch marks when you have kids. Some women have kids and don't get stretch marks.

Because they have more elastin in their skin...did you ever got to a biology class? I grew My bones and muscles grew quicker than my skin so it got a little stretched. I used to have a bit of puppy fat and a bit of a tum and it left with me with this. I've also got some on my hips and bum. Even some on my arm pits – wanna check those bad boys out? Right stand up.

Stand up.

Turn around.

Look. Look at that on your hip. Stretch marks. Guys get them too.

And I don't see any babies coming out of you.

What about these freckles? Have these distracted you from me taking my kit off? They've been there for bloody ages too.

If you want an actual war wound this one, here on my elbow, this is why I have a fear of bikes – I fell off my bike when I was ten into a rose bush. Head first, rolled right off like a circus performer. My best mate thought it was hilarious and pulled me back out ankle first.

Or this one here, look at this bad boy. I was dancing on a table in Marbella trying to get free drinks. Slipped off, fell arse over tit and cracked my head on a railing. Still got a free bottle of Grey Goose.

But this, there was no trauma, no hospital visit, just life. I lived and grew and these little lines came a long for the ride. I don't think I ever spoken this much about a squiggly line on my belly.

No you can't touch it!. Trust me, you're not touching anything now.

It doesn't make me damaged goods. It makes me human. Just like your little booty stretch marks – how do I know you haven't had butt implants and me checking your bum out in those suit trousers is all a horrid illusion?

I'll order you're a taxi babe. My arms have grown long enough to reach for my phone and get you one.

**Wined and Dined**

**by Steph Lacey**

**Genre: Comedy**

**Age: Any**

**Accent: Any**

**Length: 1 minute**

*Gemma is well and truly fed up of online dating apps.*

Here we go...again! That one seemed alright as well. I don't wanna see your massive dick! I mean, I'm not saying I want my fella to have a cocktail sausage or anything, but don't thrust the thing in my face the first time I set eyes on ya and I certainly don't want a self-portrait of the fucker! Anyway, I've got this café where I take all my dates because it meets all my criteria. And it's proper low key as well 'cause no one I know really goes there. But even that's starting to backfire on me a bit now, 'cause the staff keep looking at me like 'oh my god, not another fella', but you've gotta kiss your frogs haven't you? The way I'm going though, I'm gonna have to start buying shares in Chapstick, because I haven't even been upgraded to pauper, let alone Prince! I did meet this one guy though and he seemed lovely...*seemed.*

We went out for a drink and I went back to his...don't judge me, I'm a modern woman and I've got needs. But he turned out to be just like the rest, and I'm not even saying I wanna be

wined and dined, I just don't wanna be fucked...and chucked!

Printed in Great Britain
by Amazon